DISASTER
MASTER PLAN

DISASTER MASTER PLAN

Prepare Or Despair-It's *Your* Choice

Lorraine Holmes Milton

To order additional copies of this book, contact:
Xlibris Corporation
1-888-795-4274
www.Xlibris.com
Orders@Xlibris.com
128428

I am dedicating this book to the American People.

Question: Do you know where your DPK is?®

Please prepare for disaster and obtain a Disaster Preparedness Kit (DPK).

Hurricane

Superstorm

Tornado

Flooding

Fire

Earthquake

In September 2004, Hurricane Ivan slammed the Gulf Coast, particularly Pensacola, Florida, where my family and I resided. It was devastation beyond words, chaos, turmoil, and disaster that was unmentionable. There were screaming babies, crying while their parents waited in line in the blistering heat from the sun for Federal Emergency Management Agency (FEMA) to graciously give food (Meals Ready To Eat [MRE]), water, ice, powdered milk, baby formula, diapers, and the basic necessities needed during and after a disaster.

There were trees toppled on rooftops, houses were caved in, cars and vans were dented by the trees and other debris fallen on them, bridges collapsed, roads were blocked, and the water system compromised. We were encouraged to boil the water to purify it before drinking it. There was a power outage; therefore, the water couldn't be boiled. I thought it would be nice if I had purchased some water purification tablets or chlorine bleach to purify the water. (Note: The water purification formula is available on American Red Cross [ARC] Web site www.redcross.org)

The next year, another gigantic hurricane struck the Gulf Coast. In August 2005, Hurricane Katrina slammed into the Gulf Coast, devastating the entire region, especially flooding New Orleans, including near Parishes and Mississippi. To date, February 2013, the region has not fully recovered. The main devastation was caused by the breach of the levees—the U.S. Army Corps of Engineers has rebuilt the levees to hurricane proof, however, many residents who had relocated did not return. Thousands of the residents relocated to Houston and surrounding communities.

In 2012, Hurricane Sandy changed into Super Storm Sandy before plunging into the East Coast, affecting New York, New Jersey, Connecticut, Maine, and surrounding areas. The residents were without power for several weeks, and many did not have the basic essentials and disaster supplies to sustain themselves during that time. In some communities, there were a mandatory evacuation notice—some residents did not heed the evacuation warning and were caught in a very dangerous situation.

Listen: When the authorities issue a mandatory evacuation warning, *evacuate—just do it*! Just like Bill Cosby and Alvin F. Poussaint M.D., says in their book, *Come On People*. I know we can do better than this—act responsibly for ourselves and our families.

This book, *Disaster Master Plan: Prepare or Despair—It's* Your *Choice*, is the first book of several books to be written on this subject. The main focus of this book is to list different types of disaster preparedness kits and where to purchase the items needed to prepare for a hurricane or disaster. I want my fellow citizens to be prepared for any disaster as well as they can be prepared. Pre and post disaster of three to five days planning is the main focus.

I have researched many books and Web sites, and this information is subject to change at any time, therefore, the reader should contact the source to verify if the printed information is still accurate. Many companies start new businesses, and others will go out of business.

The intention is to give you, the consumer and fellow citizen, a quality book with the best information you can use to prepare for a disaster. Book 2 will be aimed at long-term disaster planning, disaster bunkers, and underground food storage bins. Long-term disaster planning is needed and this information is used for planning purposes just in case a disaster devastates your region for weeks to months. I truly hope this will *never* happen, however, we *must* be prepared.

I want to let everyone know the importance of preparing for a disaster. Most people prepare to eat, go to school, go to work, go to church, go to the beach, go to wherever (I'm sure you get the point). Why not prepare for a *disaster*?

FEMA and The Red Cross cannot do everything for everyone and should not be expected to do everything! Citizens should be expected to prepare for their family's needs; they should not expect handouts for any item that we can purchase, in advance, ourselves. Now let me clarify, of course, there will be a minimal amount of people, such as the elderly, the disabled, those with limited income, students, etc., who do not have the ability to become prepared. There are many groups who will need bona fide assistance, and there are others who did not prepare and will become indignant when the government is not quick to respond and give them items that should have been purchased in advance. FEMA is doing a tremendous job in disaster-preparedness planning. Sometimes, they may have items on back order because they assisted people that really were not in a "real need" (should have been prepared in advance). This is a "false" handout because it is not right. The people in true need are left out in the cold without the needed supplies.

When FEMA hands out supplies, maybe they should take a quick survey of who has the resources to purchase, in advance, of the disaster and those who have a true need. I'm sure the disaster line will become much shorter.

The Disaster Resources List will have information to build your disaster kit.

FEMA has outstanding programs to assist you in preparing for a disaster. Please go to the Web site www.fema.gov to get disaster information. ARC sells disaster kits on their Web site; please go to www.redcross.org for more information on disaster planning and how to order a disaster kit. If you are caring for a disabled person or special needs family member, you should request from their doctor an extra supply of medication to store in the kit. If you have a baby, stock up on baby food, milk, diapers, wipes, clothes, blankets, etc. Small children will be afraid, so please pack toys, teddy bears, and games, so they will feel loved, and warm clothes and appropriate items for their comfort. Question: If you had only fifteen minutes to gather all your necessary items for you and your family, what would you pack? Would you be ready? The answer is, probably not! I say this because I have attended many seminars and talked to many attendees, and about 1 percent, or less, say that they are ready and have a disaster kit standing by just in case of an emergency or disaster. Many say they carry their disaster kit in their car/van trunk.

There are many companies that sell quality disaster kits, and I am giving you the information where to purchase them.

America's weatherman Al Roker has a message for you, dated February 14, 2014, Addressed to Coalition Members by Ready. Gov, it reads; "As part of the nation's largest online resource for preparedness, it's easy for us to forget that not everyone is thinking about preparedness. Did you know that while 60% of Americans agree it's important to all Americans to be prepared for natural or man-made disasters, only 15% believe they are prepared for a disaster situation? If this statistic is alarming to you, you are not alone. Good news: you can help to change it. Read on.

Al Roker Reveals 3 Steps To Weathering A Disaster

In part . . ." We know from our experience the incredible power of advertising to impact American lives and believe these PSAs will play a significant role in raising awareness of these critically important issues, while entertaining audiences" said Peggy Conlon, president and CEO of the Ad Council. Al personally selected this social issue among the Ad Council's 50 national campaign and participated in brainstorming sessions with ad agency Leo Burnett to help inform the creative. The segment is designed to encourage Americans to take steps to prepare in advance of emergencies in three steps. 1) Make a kit; 2) Practice drills, and 3)) Know your area.

How can you help spread the word about the PSA and help others prepare?" Go to www.ready.gov to read the entire article and see video and survey.

DISASTER INFORMATION

This information was taken from USAA, the USAA Educational Foundation, "Preparing for and Recovering from a Disaster," pages 7-8.

Food and Water

Three-day supply of water, one (1) gallon daily for each family member. Replace every three months.

Three-day supply of nonperishable food (for each family member). Replace prior to expiration date.

- Manual can opener and utensils
- Camp stove with fuel or other nonelectric cooking devices
- Paper or plastic plates and bowls
- Battery-powered or hand-crank radio and extra batteries
- Copy of disaster plan and important phone numbers
- Cell phone, extra battery, and charger
- Laptop, extra battery, and charger
- Whistle to signal for help
- Waterless hand cleaner
- Antibiotic ointment
- Adhesive bandages in assorted sizes
- Eye wash solution

- Pain relievers for adults and children
- Sterile dressings
- Thermometer
- Insect repellent and sunscreen
- Hygiene products, such as soap and toothpaste
- Tweezers
- Petroleum jelly or other lubricants
- Estate planning documents—will(s), power of attorney, trusts, medical directives, etc.
- Licenses, passports, birth certificates, marriage certificates, Social Security cards, military records
- ATM or debit card and bank and credit card information
- Homeowners, renters, auto, life and medical insurance policy information
- Inventory lists, photo or disk of possessions

Special Needs

- Infant formula, baby food, diapers, and other supplies
- Prescription medications (one week supply) and copies of prescriptions
- Prescribed medical supplies, such as glucose or blood pressure monitoring devices
- Eyeglasses, contact solutions, and contact case
- Items for family members with special needs
- Items for elderly family members

PET Needs

- Three-day supply of food and water
- Leash and collar with identification date of rabies vaccination
- Immunization records
- Pet carrier or wire cage

Other Basics

- Flashlight with extra batteries
- Fire extinguisher (inspect monthly)
- Masks to help filter dust
- Work gloves
- Sanitation supplies, such as moist towelettes
- Plastic sheeting and duct tape to create a shelter
- Wrench or pliers to turn off utilities
- Local maps
- Change of clothing and shoes for each individual
- Include coats, scarves, and gloves for cold climates
- Extra set(s) of vehicle keys
- Cash and coins for one to two weeks
- Plastic garbage bags
- Chlorine bleach and instructions for disinfecting
- Emergency supplies for your vehicle

To read the entire pamphlet, please visit www.usaafoundation.org.

I founded the DPK Company LLC after Hurricanes Ivan and Katrina. I made several Disaster Preparedness Kits (DPKs) and wanted to sell them. During a doctor's visit, I approached Samina Ansar Ghazi, MD, of Farmington Hills, Michigan, and asked if she needed a disaster kit. Dr. Ghazi stated, of course, "I want to buy a disaster kit for my family." During an appointment to complete my income taxes, I asked my certified public accountant (CPA) Benjamin Holloway of Southfield, Michigan if he wanted to purchase a disaster kit, and he said yes. I call both Dr. Ghazi and Mr. Holloway the smartest people in the world because they know the value of being prepared at home and at their business location.

Dr. Ghazi explained that she was traveling in Canada when a snowstorm blanketed the area. She said, she wished she had her warm blanket and other items from the disaster kit. I will always be grateful to them for purchasing my first two disaster kits.

It is very important to realize that a disaster can happen at any time. You should be prepared.

Don't be Scared—Be Prepared!

This is one of my slogans. FEMA is doing everything in their power to prepare the nation for disaster. Please go to www.fema.gov for disaster planning information.

FEMA recently started a proactive approach to disaster planning, FEMA.gov Communities.

The National Preparedness Coalition send their mailing list subscribers an updated information via e-mail to inform us about active communities that have assisted their residents in preparing for disaster.

I love this approach because it helps me to be proactive in my disaster planning thinking.

These are some of the topics discussed on the e-mails:

- January 19, 2013: What's New in National Preparedness Coalition.
- Emergency Plan for Elderly Homes Orientation
- Pet Caretakers Learn Pet First Aid and CPR
- Global Cooling Capabilities of CryoRain Inc.
- Pet Disaster Planning
- 2013 Statewide CERT Conference (California)

Another FEMA e-mail:

- January 18, 2013: What's New in National Preparedness Coalition
- Emergency Plan for Elderly Homes Orientation
- Functional Exercise Planning Meeting
- Pet Caretakers Learn Pet First Aid and CPR
- Pet Disaster Planning
- CERT backpack addition idea
- Clothing donations to Sandy victims

Please go to the FEMA Web site to add your e-mail to the list. If you or your communities are having disaster planning activities, FEMA would like to know.

The American Red Cross assists individuals and families in disaster too. Go to www.redcross.org.

You can view disaster preparedness kit information and purchase your disaster kit. It is not morally right or may be illegal to view these lists and then create your own list from this information. These businesses are in business to make a profit, and they should be respected.

Disaster Preparedness Kit Information List

DPK Company LLC sells Disaster Preparedness Kit (DPK)

Standard Product Inventory List

E-mail lomilt@aol.com to order. Enter "Disaster Kit" in subject line.

1. Radio, crank (1)
2. First aid kit
3. Power inverter (100 watts or higher)
4. Gas mask (1)
5. Dust mask (1)
6. Life Vest (1)
7. Flashlight, Crank or Solar (1)
8. Blanket (1)
9. Food: nutrition food bars (6)
   Turkey Spam (2, with a small box of crackers), fruit, small can (2)
10. Water (1 gallon)
11. Water purification tablets (1 bottle)
12. Pliers (1)
13. Scissors

14. Disinfectant spray (1)
15. Document holder
16. Notebook
17. Ink pen
18. Duffel bag

Lorraine's Creations is a craft company that I founded in 2012. I had a good idea: the Towelpad/Blanketpad, which is patent pending. The terms Towelpad and Blanketpad are used interchangeably; they are versatile, durable, comfortable, and high-quality two-sided blankets that can be used for disaster preparedness kits, crafting activities, beach trips, camping, games, baby diaper changer pad, enuresis (bedwetting)—the possibilities are endless. For more information and to order, go to www.etsy.com/shop/lomiltdomilt or contact me through e-mail: lomilt@aol.com, to order—enter "Blanketpad" in subject line.

Included in an e-mail, Sandra Bruce stated, in part, "No matter where you are headed this summer, all you need to make the trip complete is a Blanketpad from Lorraine's Creations (Etsy). Lorraine's Creations designs personal Towelpads and Blanketpads that are amazingly durable and incredibly versatile. The possibilities are endless!"

If all households purchased a disaster kit in 2013, then the US economy will drastically improve creating much revenue.

The main point: buy a disaster kit *NOW!*

Today, as I continue to write this book, *Disaster Master Plan: Prepare or Despair*—It's Your *Choice,* September 2012, the *Good Morning America* show displayed a devastating flooding disaster in Las Vegas. A dam had broken and ferociously flooded houses up to the roof levels in many cases.

The residents that purchased a disaster kit probably put on their life vest. Remember to always put your life vest on first and then attend to your family members. The flooding was treacherous, and the water was gushing; however, a life vest is better than nothing. We cannot get completely prepared for *all* disasters; however, we can become as prepared as is practical.

This means taking *action now,* and not when the hurricane is approaching or when the hurricane season arrives (June 1 to November 30) each year. We should not wait until the National Oceanic Atmospheric Administration (NOAA) announces that a severe hurricane is imminent and on the way to your area. It would be too late by then because most stores will probably be sold out of essential supplies, for instance, nonperishable food, water, batteries, and other disaster-related supplies.

Please listen:

Prepare Now

For

a

Disaster

One of the best gifts you can give your family with the exception of "blood" is a disaster kit that works for you and your family.

If you reside in Florida, your disaster kit will be slightly different than a person residing in Michigan. In warm climates, you'll need a portable ice maker, and in cold climates, you'll need warm blankets and/or a Blanketpad.

Remember Hurricane Ivan that wreaked havoc on the Gulf Coast, including Pensacola, Florida, where I was cleaning up debris and mopping floors, etc. I am a service-disabled veteran and was in a tremendous amount of pain, so the family decided to drive to my best friend's house in Springhill, Louisiana, Dr. Gerome and Mrs. Mary Thompson. We were relieved to be in a "normal" environment. We are so grateful that they opened their home and were so hospitable. In Pensacola, there were blue plastic tarps on many houses and battered trees the streets. There were sounds of hammers, chisels, and electric motors where the community was trying to repair their homes and doing cleanup. Most of the Pensacola residents were affected, and you could see the sadness on the faces and the community was very tired and it began to show—they stood strong.

Many families did not evacuate even though there were mandatory evacuation. Please don't let the number of the hurricane affect your decision to evacuate because, in some cases, a Category 1 hurricane can bring damage as debilitating as a Category 2 or 3—the damage occurs in different ways, i.e., flooding, property damage, etc.

Please take the necessary steps to ensure that your family is safe.

Disaster Resource List

1. FEDERAL EMERGENCY MANAGEMENT ADMINISTRATION (FEMA)

www.fema.gov

- Disaster planning and more

2. AMERICAN RED CROSS (ARC)

www.redcross.org

- Disaster Kits, Emergency Radio, Water Purification Tablets, and more

3. DPK COMPANY LLC

lomilt@aol.com

- Disaster Kits and Blanketpads and more.

4. ULINE SHIPPING SUPPLY SPECIALISTS

www.uline.com

- First Aid Kits, Antibiotic Ointment, Disinfectant Spray, Clorox Bleach, Cleaning Supplies, and more

5. COLEMAN'S MILITARY SURPLUS

www.colemans.com

- Gas Masks, First Aid Kits, Disaster Blankets, Flashlights (crank/solar), Food—MREs (Meals Ready To Eat) and more.

6. RADIO SHACK

www.radioshack.com

- Emergency Radio, Flashlight (crank), and more

7. SEARS

www.sears.com

- Disaster Kits, Power Inverter, Emergency Radio, Flashlight with USB port, and more

8. LORRAINE'S CREATIONS

www.etsy.com/shop/lorrainescreations
lomilt@aol.com

- Towelpad and Blanketpad with matching pillows and more

9. USAA

www.usaafoundation.org

- To order free copy of pamphlet, "Preparing For and Recovering From A Disaster," and more

10. TARGET

www.target.com

- Food, water, nutrition bars, nutrition shakes, First Aid Kits, Antibiotic Ointment, Flashlight (crank/solar), Chlorine Bleach, Disinfectant Spray, batteries, blankets, and more

11. NORTHERN TOOL AND EQUIPMENT-

www.northerntool.com

- Power Inverters, Flashlight (crank), Generators, Batteries, and more

12. ACADEMY OF SPORTS

www.academyofsports.com

- Life Vests, Life Jackets and Life Preservers, and more

13. WALMART

www.walmart.com

- Food, Water, Nutrition Bars, Life Vest, Life Jacket, First Aid Kit, Disinfectant Spray, Antibiotic Ointment, Flashlights (crank/solar), Chlorine Bleach, Blankets, and more

14. DOLLAR GENERAL STORES

www.dolgencorp.com

- Food, Water, Blankets, Antibiotic Ointment, Flashlights, Disinfectant Spray, and more

15. AMAZON

www.amazon.com

- Disaster Kits, First Aid Kits and Books, Flashlight (crank/solar), and more

16. LOWES

www.lowes.com

- Flashlights (crank/solar), Batteries, Charcoal/Gas Grill, Matches, Lighter, and more

17. HOME DEPOT

www.homedepot.com

- Flashlights (Dual Power), Batteries, Pliers, and more

18. ACE

www.ace.com

- Pliers, Power Inverters, Batteries, Whistles, and more

19. WALGRENS

www.walgrens.com

- First Aid Kit, Chlorine Bleach, First Aid Kit, Antibiotic Ointment, and more.

20. CVS

www.cvs.com

- First Aid Kits, Antibiotic Ointment, Flashlights, and more

21. SAM'S CLUB

www.samsclub.com

- Disaster Kits (Year's Supply of Food), Food (a YEAR's supply), Water, First Aid Kit, Antibiotic Ointment, Chlorine Bleach, USB Universal Chargers, Power Inverters, Generators, and more

22. COSTCO

www.costco.co

- Food, Water, First Aid Kits, Antibiotic Ointment, Chlorine Bleach, Power Inverters, (Supplies arrive daily) and more. BUY NOW!

23. BE PREPARED.COM

www.beprepared.com

- Flashlights (crank), Emergency essentials, Pantry Freeze-Dried Foods, Year's Supply of Food, Dehydrated, Food Storage in Cans, and more

24. HID COUNTRY

www.hidcountry.com

- Flashlights LED, Zoom, Seat belt Extender, and more

25. GOAL ZERO

www.goalzero.com

- Solar Generator, Mobile Chargers, Portable Solar Chargers, and more

26. ALL COMMUNICATIONS NETWORK (ACN)

www.lorrainemilton.acnibo.com
lorrainemilton.acndirect.com

- Mobile Communications Devices, Cell Phones, Chargers, Hot Spot (Use your computer Internet anywhere in the country), and more

27. NEXTAG

www.nextag.com

-Two-person, Three-Day Emergency Disaster Kit, American Red Cross Emergency SmartPack.

28. EBAY

www.ebay.com

- Flashlights (crank/solar), Disaster Kits, and more

29. MAGLITE

www.maglite.com

- Maglite Flashlight Manufacturer—LED Flashlights and more

30. SUREFIRE FLASHLIGHTS

www.surefire.com

- Surefire manufactures powerful LED lights and candescent lights, wrist lights, head lamps. They sell batteries and more

31. 21ST CENTURY GOODS

www.2lcenturygoods.com

- Flashlights and more

32. EARTH TECH PRODUCTS

www.earthtechproducts.com

- Flashlights (crank), Emergency Radio, and more

33. OVERSTOCK.COM

www.overstock.com

- Emergency Radio, Flashlight (crank), and more

34. BROOKSTONE

www.brookstone.com

- Flashlights and more

35. SURVIVAL GUIDE

www.survivor-gear-first-aid-product.com

- Emergency Radios, Emergency Water, Emergency Food, and more

36. NITROPAK

www.nitropak.com

- Emergency Radio and more

37. WEATHER RADIO STORE

www.weatherradiostore.com

- Emergency Radio, NOAA, Weather Radios, and more

38. HEARTLAND AMERICA

www.heartlandamerica.com

- Emergency Radio and more

39. C. CRANE

www.ccrane.com

- Emergency Radio, Solar Radio, and more

40. RED CROSS STORE

www.redcrossstore.com

- Disaster Preparedness Kit, American Red Cross Power NOAA Weather Radio, American Red Cross Solar Link, Eton Emergency Radio, and more

41. ETON CORPORATION

www.eton.com

42. AMATEUR RADIO EMERGENCY SERVICE (ARES)—ARRL

www.arrl.org

- The Amateur Radio Emergency Services (ARRSW) consists of licensed amateurs who have voluntarily registered their qualification and equivalent with the local ARES leadership for communications duty in the public service when disaster strikes.

(This information was taken from Google search results.)

43. CHICAGO EMERGENCY CLOSING CENTER, SCHOOL CLOSINGS—WGN RADIO

www.wgn.com

- Chicago's Emergency losing Center, the place to check if your school or business is closed.

(This information was taken from Google search results.)

44. HAMMACHER

www.hammacher.com

45. OREGON SCIENTIFIC

www.oregonscientic.com

- Emergency Portable Weather Radio and more

46. LL BEAN

www.llbean.com

- Emergency Weather Radio (crank/solar), and more

47. HAM UNIVERSE

www.hamuniverse.com

- Ham Radio, Emergency Power, Wind, Solar, Emergency Generator, Survivors Buyers Guide, and more

48. SHARPER IMAGE

www.sharperimage.com

- Emergency Radio (crank) and more

49. RADIO ABOUT.COM

www.radioabout.com

- Radios for emergencies and disasters

50. EMERGENCY ALERT SYSTEM (EAS) PUBLIC SAFETY AND FCC

www.fcc.gov/pshs/cas

- The system also may be used by state and local authorities to deliver important emergency information, such as AMBER alerts and weather information targeted to specific areas.

(Information taken from Google search results.)

Please search Google for Amateur Radio Emergency Services in your area. The Internet had certain specific areas under "Amateur Radio Emergency Services"; however, they were limited amount of geographical area radio services.

If the author listed those specific services in specific areas and not all areas, then there would be controversy and questions, such as why did the author list some areas and not others.

51. INTERAMER

www.interamer.com

- Gas masks and more

52. APPROVED GAS MASK

www.approvedgasmasks.com

53. CAMPING SURVIVAL

www.campingsurvival.com

- Gas masks and more

54. DISASTER PREPAREDNESS

www.disasterpreparedness.com

- Eton Emergency Radio (crank)

55. GIFTS.COM

www.gifts.com

- Eton Emergency Radio (crank)

56. COURSES AND TRAINING

www.arrl.org/courses-training

- Amateur Radio Emergency Service (ARES) teams offer instruction for the introduction to Emergency communication.

57. EMERGENCY TALK RADIO

www.healthradio.net

911—Emergency Talk Radio, brought to you by the American College of Emergency Physicians, provides important information about life in the ER and how it affects you or your loved ones.

Some of the best medicine is being practiced in America's emergency rooms.

(Information taken from Google search results.)

58. EMERGENCY RADIO PROCEDURES

www.uscg.mil/pvs/docs/mayday.pdf

59. HACH COMPANY

www.hach.com

- Bleach, Water Purification

60. QUAKE KARE

www.quakekare.com

- Emergency Drinking Water Germicidal Tablets. A bottle of fifty tablets purifies twenty-five gallons of water.

61. JC PENNEY

www.jcp.com

- blankets and more

62. SALVATION ARMY (SATERN)

www.satern.org

- Emergency Radio Network

63. EDS (EMERGENCY DISASTER SYSTEM)

www.edisastersystems.com

- Food, water, First Aid Kits, Emergency Survival Kits, Safety Vests, Lights, Emergency Radios, Generators, and more

Seventy-Two-Hour Survival Kit: Two Person, Three-Day Emergency Supply Kit

Kit Contents:

- 2   -Emergency Food Bars (2,400 Calories)
- 24 -Packets Emergency Drinking Water (4.227 oz. each)
- 2   -Emergency Blankets
- 4   -Twelve-Hour Light Sticks
- 30 -Antiseptic Towelettes
- 2   -Packet Pocket Tissues
- 14 -Large Plastic Bags
- 1   -Carrying Pack with Logo
- 2   -Hygiene Kits
- 2   -Emergency Ponchos
- 2   -Whistles
- 1   -Tube Test
- 1   -First Aid Guide

First Aid Essentials

- 2   -Coldpack Instant Chemical
- 2   -Triangular Bandages (Arm Sling)
- 2   -Pair of Disposable Gloves
- 2   -Elastic Bandages -3" x 4.5 yards
- 1   -First Aid Kit

Note: Rolling Backpack only comes in Red.

My Food Storage
Long Term Food Storage

www.myfoodstorage.com to order.

Details

Our essential survival kits contain a variety of everyday gear along with a two-week supply of our food for one adult. For two adults, the food will last one week. These lightweight backpacks are great for grabbing on the go and are pre-packed for easy transportation and sorting. Take them camping, or store them some place in case of an emergency. Weight—16 lbs.

Each kit includes the following:

Packages of pocket Tissue (6)
4-in-1 Dynamo Flashlight (6)
Deck of Playing Cards (1)
Waterproof Matches (50)
Water Bags (2)
Leather Palm Work Gloves (1)
Thirty-six-Piece Bandages Kit (1)

Water Filtration Bottle (1)
Portable Stove (1)
Stove Fuel Tablets (16)
Metal Fork (1)
Knife and Spoon (1)
Sierra Cup (1)

Wise Emergency Food Supply (forty-four servings) including:

Savory Stroganoff
Chili Macaroni
Creamy a la King and Rice
Pasta Alfredo
Creamy Pasta and Veg Rotini
Teriyaki and Rice
Creamy Tomato Basil Soup
Hearty Tortilla Soup
Apple Cinnamon Cereal
Brown Sugar and Maple Cereal
Crunchy Granola

Emergency LifeLine.Com

www.emergencylifeline.com to order.

Household Emergency Kits

Survival Kit 1

One Person—Three Days

This kit was designed for minimum support for two persons in three days.

It includes items necessary for survival but does not include items necessary for survival but does not include every item you might find necessary or desirable during an emergency. You are encouraged to carefully access your specific personal needs and supplement the kit accordingly. Consider adding the following items: critical medications, feminine hygiene supplies, pencil and tablet, additional plastic bags, extra clothing, and particularly some comfortable shoes. This kit is packed in a sturdy backpack for hands-free mobility. There is room in the backpack for some additional supplies.

Gear	Qty	Description
Food	1	Emergency Food Bar 3,600 Calories
Water	24	Emergency Food Pouches 4.2 Ounces per Pouch
SAR	1	Mylar-Type Emergency Blanket
Gloves	1	Palm Gloves, Pair
Dusk Mask	1	
Medical	6	Benzalkonium Chloride Antiseptic Wipes
Antibiotic Ointment	2	0.5 g Packets
Gauze Sponges	4	2 x 2, Sterile (2 Twin Packs)
ABD Tendersorb,	2	5 x 9", Sterile
	2	Gauze Rolls 3 x 4" 1 yard, sterile
	11	Tape, 1/2" x 10 yards
	2	butterfly Bandages
	2	Finger Splints
	1	First Aid Guide
	1	Tweezers
	1	Plastic scissors with Stainless Steel
Type	2	Latex Exam Gloves, Single Lighting Twelve-Hour Green Light Sticks
	1	Standard Flashlight Alkaline D-Cell Batteries
Comm	1	AM/FM Radio with Batteries
	1	Whistle
Hygiene	3	Infections Waste Bags With Ties
	1	Personal Tissues Pack
	12	Pre-moistened Towelettes
	1	Toothbrush and Pa

DisasterRecoveryStore.com

www.disasterrecoverystore.com to order

Eight-Person "Buckeye Style" Emergency Kit

Our eight-person "buckeye style" preparedness kit comes in a rugged weather resistant plastic container for portability. All of our multiperson kits also include our Dynamo Radio Flashlight that never needs batteries. We also have optional toilet seats (see related items) that fit on top of the bucket. Every disaster kit we sell contains a minimum of three days' worth of food and water the same supplies used by disaster relief agencies. Anything perishable has a five-year shelf life from the date of manufacture—four times longer than average supermarket supplies. What's more, we keep track of remaining life of your supplies and alert you when it's time to replenish perishable items. Kits available for size family.

Kit Contents:

- (8) 3,600-Calorie Food Bars
- (48) Aqua Blox Drinking Water
- (1) Dynamo Radio and Flashlight Crank Powered 3-LED AM/FM Radio and Cell Phone Charger
- (8) Thermal Blankets—designed to reflect 90 percent of your body heat
- (8) Light Sticks—twelve hours of light in an instant

- (1) Emergency Ponchos and Hoods—protect yourself from the rain
- (1) Safety Whistle—Blow loud for immediate rescue attention
- (8) Dust Masks—prevents dust and germ inhalation

(8) Tissue Packs—helps maintain sanitary conditions

(1) First Aid Kit—comprehensive first aid kit packaged in a hard plastic case.

(50) Water Purification Tablets—to purify water for drinking

(1) Multifunction tool—fourteen-function stainless steel, includes screwdrivers, knives, and pliers

(25) Waterproof matches—light after getting wet

(1) Duct Tape—great for various applications

(1) Nylon Cord—sixty feet of heavy-duty nylon cord

(1) Gas shut-off wrench—safely shut off most gas valves after an earthquake

(1) Work Gloves—Heavy duty with leather palms

(1) Toilet Chemicals—maintain sanitary conditions

(6) Emergency candles—Each has five hours

(1) Tube Tent—comes with rope and instructions

(1) 3-in-1 can opener—Easy to use GI-style corporation

(8) Out-of-State Contact Cards—Keep track of loved ones and important numbers

(2) Packages in a Five—Gallon Airtight Container, additional food and water available for added days of protection

Additional person add-ons to increase the number of people protected.

Also available in sizes to support two- to eight-person families.

Food and water expires five years from the date of manufacture.

Kits4Disaster.com

Disaster Emergency Home Kits

Home Emergency Kits

Be prepared with one of our quality emergency survival kits for seventy-two-hour duration. Emergency preparedness for seventy-two hours is essential in the event of a disaster while local authorities and personnel are dealing with primary objectives. Our kits have quality components and supplies including five-year—shelf-life food and water, communication, shelter, tools, plus many more items to take care of you and your family in the event of an emergency. Great for taking along on travel to be prepared. See our emergency survival preparedness gear and equipment for an earthquake survival kit, emergency survival kit for disaster survival.

Take a look at our selection of emergency survival kits. All of our emergency home survival kit products are offered at great prices. If you are looking for a home survival emergency kit, you will find we have what you need.

Deluxe Emergency Disaster Kit Honey Bucket

Four-Person

This deluxe emergency kit in its well-known "Honey Bucket" has everything you need for seventy-two-hour emergency relief and comes in this convenient bucket that is easy to store your disaster supplies.

This disaster kit is equipped for four people.

    1   -Honey Bucket with Lid
    4   -2,400 calorie Food Bar
    4   -Solar Blanket
    24 -Pouches of Water
    4   -Dust Mask
    4   -Ponchos
    12 -Liners and Chemicals
    6   -Wet Naps
    1   -Twelve-hour light stick
    1   -Fifty-four-Piece First Aid Kit

1 -Radio/Flashlight/Siren
1 -Gas and Water Shut-Off Tool
1 -Pair Leather Palm Gloves
1 -T-5 Chemical Disinfectant
50 -Water Purification Tablets
50 -Waterproof matches
1 -Utility Knife
1 -5-in-1 Whistle
1 -Roll Duct Tape
1 -15-inch Pry Bar

WWW.READY.GOV

www.ready.gov/basic-disaster-supplies-kit to Order.

Basic Disaster Supplies Kit

A basic emergency supply kit could include the following recommended items:

- Water—one gallon of water per person per day for at least three days, for drinking and sanitation
- Food—at least a three-day supply of nonperishable food
- Battery—powered or hand crank and a NOAA

Build the Perfect Bug Out Bag: Your 72-Hour Disaster Survival Kit by Creek Stewart

Be ready when Disaster Strikes

If an unexpected emergency or disaster hits, are you prepared to leave your home fast?

You will be if you follow the advice in this book.

The book shows you how to create a self-contained disaster preparedness kit to help you survive your journey from ground zero to a safe location. Survival expert Creek Stewart details from start to finish everything you need to gather for 72 hours of Independent Survival—water, food, protection, shelter, survival tools, and so much more.

You'll find:

- A complete Bug Out Bag checklist that tells you exactly what to pack on your survival skill level.
- Photo and explanations of every item you need in your bag
- Resource lists to help you find and purchase gear
- Practice exercise that teach you how to use almost everything in your bag
- Demonstrations for multi-use items that save space and weight
- Specific gear recommendations for common disasters

The book even includes special considerations for bugging out with children, the elderly, the physically disabled, and even pets.

A disaster could strike your home at any moment. Are you prepared to face the devastating aftermath?

Protect yourself and your family by building a Bug Out Bag today! *www.ready.gov/build-a-kit* (the following information is from this Web site)

Water

Water is an essential element of survival and a necessary item in an emergency supplies kit. Following a disaster, clean drinking water may not be available. Your regular water source could be cut off or compromised through contamination. Prepare yourself by building a supply of water that will meet your family's needs during an emergency.

How Much Water Do I Need?

You should store at least one gallon of water daily just for drinking however individual needs vary depending on age, physical condition, activity, diet, and climate. To determine your water needs, take the following into account:

- One gallon of water per person per day, for drinking and sanitation.
- Children, nursing mothers and sick people may need more water.
- A medical emergency might require additional water.

If you live in a warm weather climate, more water may be necessary; in very hot temperatures, water needs can double.

Keep at least a three-day supply of water per person.

How Should I Store Water?

It is recommended you purchase commercially bottled water in order to prepare the safest and most reliable emergency water supply. Keep bottled water in its original container and do not open until you need to use it. Observe the expiration and "use by" date. Store in cool, dark place.

Author speaking: I recommend you store the water in the original one-gallon container of water that was purchased from a commercial store.

Note: If there are any contradictions, real or perceived, please adhere to FEMA guidelines.

Water Purification

(Please see the next page for Water Purification procedures)

Information from http://www.newjerusalem.com/PureWater.htm

Water Purification with Tablets

AQUATABS

Aquatabs are the world's number one water purification tablets. They are effervescent tablets which kill microorganisms in water to prevent cholera, typhoid, dysentery, and other waterborne diseases.

Aquatabs are available in a range of tablet sizes. Each tablet is formulated to treat a specific volume of water ranging from 1 to 2,500. Aquatabs are used in emergency situations and also for continuous use in households that do not have access to safe drinking water.

Aquatabs For Emergency And Disaster

Aquatabs are used by all major aid agencies, NGOs, and peacekeeping defense forces worldwide for the treatment of human drinking water in emergency situations.

Fifteen billion liters of water were treated using Aquatabs in 2008.

Please visit the Web site for pricing and ordering information http://store.shopreadyamerica.com/disaster.html.

(The following information is from this Web site www. shopreadyamerica.com)

Survival Kit (Three days/One person)

Availability: Usually ships in five to seven days.

Product Description

Get the basic life supplies in an expandable bag or box. Brought for one person for three days each kit contains one lightweight, compact blanket (size 52" x 84", which retains 90 percent of body heat and can double as a rain poncho or shelter, six individually sealed bags of fresh drinking water and one food bar that tastes like a cookie and provides all the essential vitamins and minerals. Keep one handy whenever you spend the most time. Five-year shelf life. U.S. Coast Guard approved. Bilingual packaging (English/Spanish).

Disaster Supplies

Supplies to prepare for earthquake, hurricane, tornadoes, wildfires, and other emergencies.

Emergency Space Blanket
Poncho
Bullhorn—25 Watts with Detachable microphone (1,000-Yard Range)
Multifunction Whistle
300-foot Caution Tape
Waterproof Matches
Backhand Multifunction Pliers
Manual Earthquake Wrench
Potable Shovel
50-foot Nylon Rope
4-in-1 Tool (Gas and Water)
Emergency Power Station, Four Function
Eveready Heavy-Duty Industrial Flashlight
Twelve-Hour Green Light stick
Duracell Batteries, AA size

Duracell Batteries, C Cell
Duracell Batteries, D Cell
New Millennium 400-calorie Food Bar, Assorted Flavors
2,400-Calorie Food Bar
Water Packet, 4.225 oz.

Water Box, 1.0 Liter
Water Barrel Rack System (with Barrels)
Water Barrel Rack System (without Barrels)
Fifty-five-Gallon Water Barrel
Water Purification Tablets
Water Preserver Concentrate (for fifty-five Gallons)

Product Description: Safely store emergency drinking water for five years. Eliminates replacing water every three to six months. Purifies and keeps water bacteriologically safe.

33-Piece First Aid Kit
107-Piece All-Purpose First Aid Kit
Evacu-Aid Stretcher
Triage Tags
Bio-Blue Toilet Chemicals Replacement Toilet Bags
(Replacement bags for the portable toilet)
Privacy Shelter
Six-Point Suspension Hard Hat
Protective Safety Goggles
Leather Palmed Work Gloves
Nitrile Gloves
Safety Vest
Nlosh N-95 Approved Dust Mask
Disposable Dust Mask
Automatic Gas Shut-Off Valve
QuakeProof Site Safety Kit Bag
Grab 'n Go 1 Person 1 Day Emergency Hip Pack
Grab 'n Go 3 Day Emergency Kit (one-person Bag)
Grab 'n Go 3 Day Emergency Kit (two-person Backpack)
Grab 'n Go 3 Day Essentials Emergency Kit (four-person Backpack)
Grab 'n Go 3 Day Deluxe Emergency Kit (four-person Backpack)

Survival Kit (3 days/1 person—Spanish/English)
Cat Evacuation Kit

Evacuation Essentials

Product Description

Essential supplies designed to escape the building and survive the first hours of an emergency. Provide one for every person in your facility. The evacuation essentials have a five-year shelf life.

Each Kit Contains:

1   Emergency Twelve-Hour Light stick
1   Emergency Whistle
1   Dust Mask
2   Nitrile Gloves
1   Survival Blanket
1   Pocket Tissues
1   Pair Goggles
1   Rubber Band (to attach light stick to wrist)
     Velcro Fastener (to attach to desk)

From the Author:

Sanitation

If the water is shut off, you can use a portable folding toilet with disposable bags. Be sure to purchase the bags in advance to ensure you have a good supply.

www.disastercenter.com/guide/kit.html

The following information was taken from this Web site.

Disaster Supplies Kit

Why Talk About Disaster Supplies Kit?

After a disaster, local officials and relief workers will be on the scene, but they cannot reach everyone immediately.

You could get help in hours, or it could take days. Basic services, such as electricity, gas, water, and telephone, may be cut off, or you may have to evacuate at a moment's notice. You probably won't have time to shop or search for the supplies you'll need. Your family will cope best by preparing for disaster before it strikes.

What is a Disaster Supplies Kit?

Assembling the supplies you might need following a disaster is an important part of your Family Disaster Plan. Following a disaster, having extra supplies at home or supplies to take with you in the event of an evacuation can help your family endure evacuation or home confinement.

Learn more about Disaster Supplies Kits by contacting your local emergency management agency or local American Red Cross Chapter.

Awareness Information

Involve Children In Disaster Preparedness

Ask children to help you remember to keep your kits in working order by changing the food and water every six months and replacing batteries as necessary. Children might make calendars or posters with the appropriate dates marked on them. Ask children to think of items that they would like to include in their own Disaster Supplies Kit, such as books or games or appropriate nonperishable food items.

Prepare Your Kit

Tips for Your Disaster Supplies Kit

Keep a smaller Disaster Supplies Kit in the trunk of each car. If you become stranded or are not able to return home, having some items will help you to be more comfortable until help arrives.

- Keep items in airtight plastic bags; this will help protect them from damage or spoiling.
- Replace store food and water every six months. Replacing your food and water supplies will help to ensure their freshness.
- Rethink your kit and family needs at least once a year. Replace batteries, update clothes, etc.

Ask your physician or pharmacist about storing prescription medicines . . . It may be difficult to obtain prescription medications during a disaster because stores may be closed or supplies may be limited.

- Use an easy-to-carry container for the supplies you would most likely need for an evacuation. Label it clearly. Possible containers include:
- A large covered trash container.
- A camping backpack.
- A duffel bag.
- A cargo container that will fit on the roof of your vehicle.

Disaster Supplies Kit Basics

The following items might be needed at home or for an evacuation. Keeping them in an easy-to-carry backpack or duffel bag near your door would be best in case you need to be evacuated quickly, such as in an a tsunami, flash flood, or major chemical emergency. Store your kit in a convenient place known to all family members. Kit basics are:

- Flashlight and extra batteries
- First aid kit and first aid manual
- Supply of prescription medications
- Credit card and cash
- Personal identification
- An extra set of car keys
- Matches in a waterproof containers
- Signal flare
- Map of the area and phone numbers of places you could go
- Special needs, for example, diapers or formula, prescription medicines and copies of prescriptions, hearing aid batteries, spare wheelchair battery, spare eyeglasses, or other physical needs.

If you have additional space, consider adding some of the items from your Evacuation Supplies Kit.

Evacuation Supplies Kit

Place in an easy-to-carry container the supplies you would most likely need if you were to be away from home for several days. Label the containers clearly.

Remember to include:

Disaster Supplies Kit Basics

- Three gallons of water per person
- Three-day supply of nonperishable food
- Kitchen accessories: manual can opener, mess kits or proper cups, plates, and plastic disposable utensils, utility knife, a can of cooking fuel if food must be cooked; household liquid bleach to treat drinking water; sugar, salt, pepper, aluminum foil, plastic resealable bag.
- One complete change of clothing and footwear for each family member; sturdy shoes or work boots, raingear, hat and gloves, thermal underwear, sunglasses
- Blankets or sleeping bag for each family member
- Tools and other accessories; paper, pencil, needles and thread; pliers, shut-off wrench, shovels, and other useful tools; tape, medicine dropper; whistle; plastic sheeting; small canister, ABC-type fire extinguisher; emergency preparedness manual, tube tent, compass
- Sanitation and hygiene items; toilet paper; towelette, soap, hand sanitizer, liquid detergent, feminine supplies, personal items such as shampoo, deodorant, toothpaste, toothbrushes, comb and brush, lip balm, plastic garbage bags (heavy duty), and ties (for personal sanitation uses); medium-size plastic bucket with tight lid; disinfectant; household chlorine bleach; small shovel for digging an expedient latrine
- Entertainment, such as games and books

Remember to consider the needs of very young and older family members, such as infants and elderly or disabled persons.

- For Baby: Formula, diapers, bottles, powdered milk, medications
- For Adults: Heart and high blood pressure medications, insulin, prescription drugs, denture needs, contact lenses and supplies, extra eyeglasses, and hearing aid batteries

To Build a Makeshift Toilet

Line a bucket with a garbage bag and make a toilet seat out of two boards placed parallel to each other across the bucket. After each use pour disinfectant such as bleach (one part liquid chlorine bleach to ten parts water) into the garbage bag. This will avoid infection and stop the spread of disease. Cover the bucket tightly when it is not in use.

Bury garbage and human waste to avoid the spread of disease by rats and insects. Dig a pit two to three feet deep and at least fifty feet downhill or away from any well, spring, or water supply.

www.humanesociety.org

The following information was taken from this Web site.

How to Keep Pets Safe in Natural Disasters or Everyday Emergencies

When disaster strikes, the same rules that apply to people apply to pets.

Preparation makes all the difference and if it's not safe for you, it's not safe for them. Take a few minutes to make a plan and assemble an emergency kit for yourself and your pet.

To-Do List for Protecting Your Pets in a Disaster

1. Start getting ready now

    ID your pet
    Put together your disaster kit
    Find a safe place to stay ahead of time

2. If you evacuate, take your pet

Make sure that your cat or dog is wearing a collar and identification that is up to date and visible at all times. You'll increase your chances of being reunited with a lost pet by having him or her microchipped; if your pet is adopted from a shelter or rescue organization, make sure the registration is transferred to you and is not still with the adoption group.

Put your cell phone number on your pet's tag. It may also be a good idea to include the phone number of a friend or relative outside your immediate area in case you have had to evacuate.

A basic disaster kit

- Food and water for at least five days for each pet, bowls, and a manual can opener if you are packing canned pet food. People need at least one gallon of water per person per day.

  While your pet may not need that much, keep an extra gallon on hand if your pet has been exposed to chemicals or flood waters and needs to be rinsed.

  Medications and Medical Records stored in a waterproof container and a first aid kit. A pet first aid book is also a good idea.
- Cat litter, litter scoop, garbage bags to collect all pets' waste.
- Sturdy leashes, harnesses, and carriers to transport pet safely and to ensure that pets can't escape carriers should be large enough to allow your pet to stand comfortably, turnaround and lie down. (Your pet may have to stay in the carrier for hours at a time.)

Be sure to have a secure cage with no loose objects inside it to accommodate smaller pets—who may also need blankets or towels for bedding and warmth as well as special items, depending on their species.

Current photos of you and your pets and descriptions of your pets to help others identify them in case you and your pets become separated—and to prove that they are yours once you're reunited.

Pet beds and toys

Written information about your pets' feeding schedule, medical conditions, and behavior issues along with the name and number of your veterinarian in case you have to board your pets or place them in foster care.

Other useful items include newspapers, paper towels, plastic trash bags, grooming items, and household bleach.

Find a safe place to stay ahead of time. Some communities have groups that have solely focused on providing emergency sheltering for pets, and other communities simply don't have the resources. That's why you should never assume that you will be allowed to bring your pet to an emergency shelter.

Before disaster hits, call your local office of emergency management to see if you will be allowed to evacuate with your pets and that there will be shelters that take people and their pets in your area.

And just to be safe, track down a pet-friendly safe place for your family and pets.

Find a Pet-Friendly Hotel or Motel

- Contact hotels and motels outside your immediate area to find out if they accept pets. Ask about any restrictions on number, size, and species.

  Inquire if the "no pet" policies would be waived in an emergency. Keep a list of animal-friendly places handy, and call ahead for a reservation as soon as you think you might have to leave your home. Here's an online resource for pet-friendly hotels:

  bringfido.com
  dogfriendly.com
  doginmysuitcase.com
  pet-friendly-hotels.net
  pets-allowed-hotels.com
  petswelcome.com
  tripswithpets.com

Make arrangements with friends or relatives. Ask people outside the immediate area if they would be able to shelter you and your pets—or just your pets, if necessary.

If you have more than one pet, you may need to arrange to house them at separate locations.

Consider a kennel or veterinarian's office. Make a list of boarding facilities and veterinary offices that might be able to shelter animals in disaster emergencies (include their twenty-four-hour telephone numbers).

As a last resort, ask your local animal shelter. Some shelters may be able to provide faster care or shelter for pets in an emergency. But shelters have limited resources and are likely to be stretched to their limits during an emergency.

Attention Institutions:

Please go to www.dPlan.org, and they will send you reminders to update your disaster plan. Great Web site. Please use it!

www.redcross.org

The following information was taken from this Web site.

Types of Emergency
Chemical
Drought
Earthquake
Fire
Flu
Food Safety
Heat Wave
Highway Safety
Hurricane
Landslide
Pet Safety
Poisoning
Power Outage
Terrorism
Thunderstorm
Tornado
Tsunami
Volcano
Water Safety
Wildfire
Winter Storm

CHEMICAL EMERGENCY

About Chemical Emergencies

Chemicals are a natural and important part of our environment. Even though we often don't think about it, we use chemicals every day. Chemicals help keep our food fresh and our bodies clean.

They help our plants grow and fuel our cars. And chemicals make it possible for us to live longer, healthier lives. Under certain conditions, chemicals can also be poisonous or have a harmful effect on your health. Some chemicals that are safe and even helpful in small amounts can be harmful in large quantities or under certain conditions.

Chemical accidents do happen, at home and in the community. The American Red Cross wants you to be prepared.

How You May Be Exposed To a Chemical

You may be exposed to a chemical in three ways.

- Breathing the chemical

- Swallowing contaminated food, water, or medication
- Touching the chemical, or coming into contact with clothing or things that have touched the chemical.

Remember, you may be exposed to chemicals even though you may not be able to see or smell anything unusual.

Chemical Accidents Can Be Prevented

Chemicals are found everywhere—in our kitchens, medicine cabinets, basements, and garages.

In fact, most chemical accidents occur in our homes, and they can be prevented.

Drought

A drought is a period of abnormally dry weather that persists long enough to produce a serious hydrologic imbalance, causing, for example, crop damage and shortages in the water supply. The severity of a drought depends on the degree of moisture deficiency, the duration, and the size of the affected area. Drought can be defined four ways:

Meteorological Drought—when an area gets less precipitation than normal.

Due to climate differences, what is considered a drought in one location may not be a drought in another location.

Agriculture Drought—when the amount of moisture in the soil no longer meets the needs of a particular crop.

Hydrological Drought—when the surface and subsurface water supplies are below normal.

Socioeconomic Drought—when water supply is unable to meet human and environmental needs can upset the balance between supply and demand.

Earthquake

An earthquake is a sudden, rapid shaking of the earth caused by the breaking and shifting of rock beneath the earth's surface. Earthquakes strikes suddenly without warning, and they can occur at any time of the year, day or night.

Forty-five states and territories in the United States are at moderate to very high risk of earthquake, and they are located in every region of the country.

Are You at Increased Risk from Earthquake?

Contact your local emergency management office, local American Red Cross, state geological survey, a department of natural resources for specific information about community risk. However, bear in mind:

- Mobile homes and homes not attached to their foundations are at particular risk during an earthquake.
- Buildings with foundations resting on landfill and other unstable soils are at increased risk of damages.

Home Fire

About Fire Safety and Prevention

The most effective way to protect yourself and your home from fire is to identify and remove fire hazards. Sixty-five percent of home-fire deaths occur in homes with no working smoke alarms.

During a home fire, working smoke alarms and a fire escape plan that has been practiced regularly can save lives.

BE RED CROSS READY

- If a fire occurs in your home
- *Get out, stay out and call* for help.
- Install smoke alarms on every level of your home, inside bedrooms, and outside sleeping areas. Test them every month and replace the batteries at least once a year.
- Talk with all household members about a fire escape plan, and practice the plan twice a year.

Flood

About Flood

Floods are the most costly natural disasters. Conditions that cause floods include heavy or steady rain for several hours a day that saturate the ground.

Flash flood occurs suddenly due to rapidly rising water along a stream or low-lying area. You will likely hear weather forecasters use these terms when floods are predicted in your community.

- **Flood/Flash Flood Watch**—Flooding or flash flooding is possible in your area.
- **Flood/Flash Flood Warning**—Flooding and flash flooding is already occurring or will occur soon in your area.

HEAT WAVE

About Heat Wave

In recent years, excessive heat has caused more deaths than all other weather events, including floods.

A heat wave is a prolonged period of excessive heat, generally ten degrees or more above average, often combined with excessive humidity. You will also hear weather forecasters use these terms when a heat wave is predicted in your community:

Excessive Heat Watch—Conditions are favorable for an excessive heat event to meet or exceed local Excessive Heat Warning criteria in the next twenty-four to seventy-two hours.

Excessive Heat Warning—Heat Index values are forecasting to meet or exceed locally defined warnings criteria for at least two days (daytime highs = 105 to 110 Fahrenheit).

Heat Advisory—Heat Index values are forecasting to meet locally defined advisory criteria for one to two days (daytime highs = 100 to 105 Fahrenheit).

(Please see Heat Wave Checklist)

Highway Safety

Take the Appropriate Steps to Stay Safe

If you are planning on hitting the highway, the American Red Cross offers this important information to help you get to your destination safely.

On the Highway

- Buckle up, slow down, don't drive impaired.
- Be well rested and alert.
- Use caution in work zones.
- Give your full attention to the road. Avoid distractions such as cell phones.
- Observe speed limits—driving too fast or too slow can increase your chances of being in a collision.
- Make frequent stops. During long trips, rotate drivers. If you're too tired to drive, stop and get some rest.
- Be respectful of other motorists and follow the rules of the road.
- Don't follow another vehicle too closely.
- If you plan on drinking, designate a driver who won't drink.

- Clean your headlights, taillights, signal lights, and windows to help you see, especially at night.
- Turn your headlights on as dusk approaches or if you are using your windshield wipers due to inclement weather.
- Don't overdrive your headlights.
- If you have car trouble, pull off the road as far as possible.

Prepare for the Unexpected

- Carry a Disaster Supplies Kit in your trunk.
- Pack high-protein snacks, water, a first aid kit, a flashlight, a small battery-operated radio, an emergency contact card with names and phone numbers, extra prescription medications, and important documents and information you may need.
- Let someone know your destination, your route, and when you expect to arrive. If your car gets stuck along the way, help can be sent along your predetermined route.
- Find out what disasters may occur in the place where you are traveling, especially if they are disasters you have never experienced before. Find out how you would get information in the event of a disaster (local radio systems, emergency alert systems).
- Pay attention to the weather forecast for your destination. Travel and weather Web sites can help you avoid storms and other regional challenges that could impact your safety.
- Don't let your vehicle's gas tank get too low.
- If you are taking your pet with you, there are several things you should know to make your trip more enjoyable. (Please see Pet Safety Checklist)

Take an American Red Cross Safety Course

Go to www.redcross.org to register.

Hurricane

About Hurricanes

Hurricanes are strong storms that can be life-threatening as well as cause serious property-threatening hazards such as flooding, storm surge, high winds, and tornadoes. Preparation is the best protection against the dangers of a hurricane. Know the difference between the threat levels and plan accordingly.

Hurricane Watch

Hurricane conditions are a threat within forty-eight hours. Review your hurricane plans. Get ready to act if a warning is issued, and stay informed.

Hurricane Warning

Hurricane conditions are expected within thirty-six hours. Complete your storm preparation and leave the area if directed to do so by authorities.

A hurricane is on its way. What do I do?

- Listen to a NOAA Weather Radio for critical information from the National Weather Service (NWS).
- Check your disaster supplies. Replace or restock as needed.
- Bring in anything that can be picked up by the wind (bicycles, lawn furniture).
- Close your windows, doors, and hurricane shutters. If you do not have hurricane shutters, close and board up all windows and doors with plywood.
- Turn your refrigerator and freezer to the coldest setting. Keep them closed as much as possible so that food will last longer if the power goes out.
- Turn off propane tanks.
- Unplug small appliances.
- Fill your car's gas tank.
- Create an evacuation plan with members of your household. Planning and practicing your evacuation plan minimizes confusion and fear during the event.
- Find out about your community's hurricane response plan. Plan routes to local shelters, register family members with special medical needs, and make plans for your pets to be cared for.
- Obey evacuation orders. Avoid flooded roads and washed-out bridges.
- Standard homeowners insurance doesn't cover flooding. It's important to have protection from the floods associated with hurricanes, tropical storms, heavy rains, and other conditions that impact the U.S.
- For more information on flood insurance, please visit the National Flood Insurance Program Web site at www. FloodSmart.gov.

Emergency Water Purification

Hurricane Katrina Materials

How To Clean Water

Do not try to use water that has floating material in it, water that has any odor, or water that has a dark color. These are all indications that the water is significantly contaminated and may be dangerous no matter what you do to filter it or kill bacteria. On the other hand, a little dirt in the water can be cleaned out easily and won't hurt anyone.

If the water is cloudy, the first thing to do is take out as much of the dirt as possible. If you have time, start by letting it settle. Put the water in a tall container and leave it for 12 to 24 hours. Carefully dip or pour the cleaner water at the top into another container. Clean the water as you put it in the new container by running it through a filter. The easiest filter is a coffee filter. If you don't have a coffee filter, use a paper towel or a piece of clean t-shirt material or similar cloth. Change the filter whenever it gets visibly dirty.

Once water is filtered, it is fine for using to clean things like clothing and floors. Don't use water that you wouldn't drink to wash you face, rinse your dishes or clean the kitchen.

How To Treat Drinking Water

Once you have reasonably clean water, it has to be treated before it is safe to drink. The purpose of this is to kill all the germs that may be in the water. The Federal Emergency Management Agency and the American Red Cross agree on three acceptable ways to treat drinking water: boiling, chlorine bleach, or distilling. There are some other systems that can have problems. In general, these three are the best. Distilling is not practical for large amounts of water.

Boiling

Water should be boiled for at least 3 to 5 minutes to sanitize it. Some agencies recommend boiling for 10 minutes just to be safe. If you live at high altitudes, add a minute for every 1000 feet above sea level. Remember that there will be evaporation and you probably want to cover the pot to retain as much of the water as possible. Once the water is boiled, let it cool in the same container. It can be put in storage bottles when it is cool.

Boiled water tends to taste flat because there is no air in it. You can add the air back by pouring the water back and forth between two clean containers. This will also improve the taste of stored or bottled water.

Boiling requires that there be a source of fuel and a safe way to store the water while it cools. If your kitchen is working, this is not a problem. If you are cooking over a grill or campfire, use bleach to purify the water.

If you are treating the water to cook with, do not add the food until the water has boiled for the amount of time needed to treat the water. There is no need to boil the water, cool it and then reheat it for cooking, but you may contaminate the food if the water has not boiled long enough before using it to cook. If you put food in contaminated water, it gives the germs a place to hide and they may not be killed in the amount of time needed to cook vegetables or pasta.

The biggest problem with boiling for water treatment is that you can't treat very much water at a time. Most kitchens don't have any pots bigger than 6 or 8 quarts and you can't fill them more than about half or two thirds full. Remember that boiling water is a safety issue. Even fairly small burns can make you very sick if they get infected.

Bleach Disinfection

Treating water with bleach is very effective at killing germs and it doesn't taste funny to most of us because this is basically what most city water supplies do. You need to have a bottle of plain liquid chlorine bleach and a dropper. The bleach should be 5 to 6 percent sodium hypochlorite with no preservatives and no additional ingredients. Do not use scented bleaches, color safe bleaches, powdered bleaches, or bleaches with added cleaners. You want the good old fashion stuff that smells like chlorine and burns holes in your clothes if you pour it right on them. Even this is hard to choose because it is now available in different concentrations. Ultra Clorox is a 6% solution instead of 5.25% but it is the same stuff. Keep a bottle of plain 5.25% or 6% chlorine bleach with no additives in the laundry room to use for water purification. Besides, this cleans sweat socks as well as any of the others.

To treat water with chlorine bleach, put the water in a clean container and add 16 drops of bleach for every gallon of water. Stir in the bleach and let the water stand for 30 minutes. If the water does not have a little smell of bleach, repeat the dosage of 16 drops per gallon and let it sit for another 15 minutes. If it smells of bleach now it is OK to drink. If it doesn't smell of bleach after two treatments, the water is too dirty to use. Throw it away and treat a new batch of water.

Amounts Of Bleach For Ordinary Containers

- 1 quart bottle   4 drops of bleach
- 2 liter soda bottle   10 drops of bleach
- 1 gallon jug   16 drops of bleach (1/8 tsp)
- 2 gallon cooler   32 drops of bleach (1/4 tsp)
- 5 gallon bottle   1 teaspoon of bleach

Index

To order the Blanketpad (http://www.etsy.com/shop/lomiltdomilt)
Photographer: Allister L. Holmes

To order the Blanketpad (http://www.etsy.com/shop/lomiltdomilt)
Photographer: Allister L. Holmes

www.ingramcontent.com/pod-product-compliance
Lightning Source LLC
Chambersburg PA
CBHW020335290526
45785CB00005B/2036